A

L

E

D

Andrew Wells

this edition first published in 2020

HESTERGLOCK PRESS

[[[[ ]]]]

publishing *mostly* the future facing

The Blue Room
25 Wathen Road,
Bristol
BS6 5BY
UK

for more information visit

website: hesterglock.net
twitter: @h g press
email: hesterglock@gmail.com

on *sealed*

"Intelligent, sharp, innovative and playful, Wells creates a looking-glass world and invites the reader to (re)examine the constructions of both language and self. Alive to the possibilities and falsities enacted through poetic language and form, these adept and aware poems move like water."
Petra Kamula

"Wells chews over language in a satisfyingly meticulous way, combing through assonance and etymologies until you are delivered of each poem feeling thoroughly worked out. I'm in love with the saltiness of this verse, the crunchy shingle-under-foot-ness of it all."
Anna Cathenka

"Take a deep breath before you enter this world of heather and surf – a world that is real and strange, rendered in "blue's bestest grammar". Here is poetry that is striking and thrillingly refreshing. Complete immersion is recommended."
Emily Hasler

Contents

Of He Not He   I
afloat, a boat, a boat   2
past moorland and line   3
the swans sawn saw water towers when, say it   4

SEALED

capeside   9
towards the sea   refused   I0
for the worse   II
bird by seal   I2
in the very west   I3
hats   I4
and they have been around forever   I5
seal breathes and says   I6
love   I7
seal will not brace   I9
seal and kayak   20
wherever the participle ends   2I
weary roll down   22
once   23
p.s. after a terrible beginning   25

Of He Not He

assume the cats' eyes
glean here not dulled repairing
if red and distant
over black water, water
breaking swiftly over do

by dot I do not
mean car I did to not mean
by irises of
either or leopard's aspect
do at all I mean to mean

today I will be
mean and meaning to bridges
needing closed, closing
eyes of the pride tonight read
him in red not reading dead

afloat, a boat, a boat

my contraction is in my canal by contraction I mean
I bottled mistakes never made and things were bottled
by which I mean to not say whether or not this is my
mistake or whether I mistook this canal for my own
pipeline out to sea and it occurs I dislike knowing how
locking works or if it works and whether a limit
really does extend beyond eyeline I think of shoreline
and / or a grey seal freed from me now freed again now I
have come around to the idea of this duck being dead
would it be cruel to google the bloating and buoyancy
of ducks assuming they suffered a head wound and did
not drown though I do not speak of ducklings would
it be cruel to google survival rates among orphaned ones
is there anything more important than my pain of seeing

past moorland and line

on the russet walls I do
not wish for brick paling
impaling terms &c. my
legs are not my own
I am too old even to be
a bear day long contusion
there are no eggs this side
of the moorland and line
I cross thinking I will have
an anthological boycott
the shins have it these
legs are not my legs   think

I am glad for the blue houses and the fog
rolling in here have cobwebs on me
again here run this instead
& what did I forget? I have
pocketed it.   the spare water
I have neither low tide nor eggs
nor my priorities down by
straits surfside gutted

the swans sawn saw water towers when, say it

lifted diminished
street lights I wish I could say
distinguished or that
arrival was by morning
aquamarine and the fog

of the racing stripe
holding thought again then told
for no throwing foil
when passing over skyways
not highways or a highway

likes I like that I
lost when the water tower
was directly in front of
me and distance demanded
blue's bestest grammar

SEALED

capeside

north of skiach
out the sea a foot   callous   skinned as rock
raised heel first– braced

apocalypse [this is
north of skiach, north of the kyle
yellow the sands in] this is

michael thinking
otherwise for [this is   ] ocean
rushing a shoal of herring
eels' tasering the achilles

when heather grows
inter-tarsal
lonely   up-cliff
lonely roebuck or rouge

I am he said glad we called the ferryman

before that down-poured on drive
exiting

in spume, oak-like raised up or
left up or moss upon that kept-cold vinylic heel, ever a first swim,
                                        raised above a shore-
line's album-worth of static

toward the sea   refused

pulled down is a
rip-tidal
ecology   a pause twice stolen
turns   stiffly   necked
to deflate and wave to   as brother in arms
yearned half the yearning of

alpacas heather-set back in the highlands   whose gaze
northerly and shorewise
dared to greet from a-far a figure on the sands

michael   whose own gaze is down-tilted   calling
ilex berries of a shallows' calm time of a shallows'
xylophone screws   sunlit   *so prophetic* before
each lifting
divergence becomes deep and truly charcoal over the world

for the worse

tinnitus bugs
alpacas out here for when
ululations are a tinny whistle
great scotch do
highlands
take a turn

my brother says tinnitus is all in my head
espousing deep truths like

that
hat is not a good fit
and likely
the source of all your troubles

insisting on tinnitus changes nothing early
for the love of god man lay it over your heel

bird by seal

bird as synonym for tires for bracing
intuitive of last calls for drinks as
red through skein is
dimmer over the grind of a world

breaking like a knuckleball is this wave
yearning short right short shy mid-flight

shy of a wall or
elliptical is that my bulky form carrying
a deflection
long and I or conflicted beyond the by-line

in the very west

there is something about
how high tide brought full circle and a stray
egret went and claimed he was afraid
right short they are on rock pools
even

intertidally because those trees before were hardly
sea palms whether kelp is fun to say as nap

so I have been told to go down weary in the kelp or suggest
or something if togetherness and tenderness
more than tethered-ness matter in
elevations as tight as the wave it is braced
toward then that is as well as I can put things when
home is provided   for home is still an island far from
inhabitants like seals and starfish.   for I reckon
narwhals are as close to permissibly equine as
green rocks and a white belly might be   in other words

a refusal to say wave   stallion   or the rest
because armour twice upon each
organism has withstood or grey together
underwent   very harsh tides quite
tired of pressure loss of water loss

barnacles   though   steel themselves   better than
anemones   for if barnacles if ever
rarely fight   then they cannot
not nearly
advise on issues such as
colony   water coverage   or territory   for if
long-time wed   to good rock or good seal
each barnacle   contentedly is
subjected to necrosis of alone a final sort

hats

boy   do
entrails stain the red barn close   why

wail would be the word
or
roar to   de-
note   defiance + fury + sort

an alpaca's
spit. if

sizzle like
olive oil turns   violence   into
consolation   – o/
kayy   so   you take yr   genocide   refrigerated do you?
thus scorned michael

and they have been around forever

now likeness not so
of sponge is so terrible
when krill / crustacea

for kale are chosen even
in approximation uniformly sponge is
not one far over
if symmetrical fangs in no aspect
symmetrical besides carnivorousness
hovering it is really not so bad

over vegetable plots
ready-prepared in quadrats other than

soon
to be sponge dying beached
or inked or bleached other than very soon I
picture sponge, stirring coarse

seal takes a breath and says

sunshine is not
awash nor upon   anemones
leaf   dunes   I call coral
the woodwork   I am corrected

and I do believe   set back in the chippy air
is a force for good lungs   neither in rawness nor
rioting palettes   because

i do not care of those notions

great waves or small waves or stratus   because I care   I care
only and I care completely   great palm to great palm

love

from north of crieff north of skiach upon
rock upon peninsula up-
on a rock
might a lighthouse be a flare that stolen

cries out for another('s) safe passage through
rocks off the peninsula   they said
it was cats' eyes   or an
equivocation so called thoracic
for its connotations of cracked and stretched
floundering besides   essential as the coastline

to which or to whom or
of which seal cries *would there were*

causeway for I cannot swim that far without
roadway and railway and double the fins   though   maybe
it is a butcher's
crime to make this   a re-
claimation
if not simply making claim to make or
engineer connection between
the sea both sides of which
high-time and higher tide reject—   then

coming up is seal   belly a sheet grey like
rain that scotch mist or mizzle
is enough to make shiver
each one issuing note
that what each were crying after is
high line of landform

shoaling a wave   and each cried out

even this is not quite what was forgotten
and nor is a middling islet if to middle is to muddle
lit by the flare of a lighthouse of the western column

seal will not brace

sand piper his own
each to back pocket mischief
alibi kept like under a wing

why ever
is the alibi nurtured
lower and lowered and
lowing when between

seal and bird
is a cow fattened on
great moons or quiet
highs, beady to the dire

end as I look for
new gulls sometimes reading eyes
dark red, the white gulls' caw guttural too

seal and kayak

wake so on hallows'
all I never considered
spending time by shore

wherever the participle ends

it has been insisted / that smoker blood
sets in my blood when orca's tooth

incisor or this isn't a rabbit poem / canine or (?)
than a car or wave down faster crashing and this extent of
                                                    no good

being heavier than one   if static
leaves static behind my shore
oxy-something will insist upon possessives' use
downplaying the insecurity of an elephant's breath

owing to another / there
roils the spraining wave

bold against wrist against flipper aghast I nearly said ripper
like perhaps I dared and do and am so pierced that
underwater I think I tricked the second person into thinking I'm
bright as a
button
easy now – I do fade – & tighten the upper back against
real tides / real rip tides /
saw   or could have seen me   in undertow dear badly gnashed
                                                    seal

weary roll down

tricked when I was by rocks
in like of herring
elegant it seemed

to roll as if on the slope
of a park and instead of geese

or mallards it signified
an impossible
roaring of elephant
seals or a walrus joking

about yellowing tusks in an all-too-
natural light

herring has become as my food
often is worn as I am
worn by
loving coast to coast and a set of dentures loving coast

to cast and a long canine dies
on me blackened in my sleep

when I go fresh on
a choppy mission in error
this is known as (acci)dental waters
every time a walrus
roars the colour of his tusk it's a good time for
speaking of a wind cutthroat between downpours.

once

two alpacas were
holding   less intertarsal than hoofwise
evergreens between

only themselves   + under-hoof
not holding more held
lightly to find let us imagine
yarrow good for

tendons on the malleolus   raised altostratus when
each new leg is quite
lassoed quite violent
everyday + this
view
isn't
strictly ours   like
it's true that
out by   that half-mirror   one falls down
now heather-set as the pane greys up the pines

if in lasso   or looped
not that I overthink of it

tenderness would wait pinch-cheeked in the brusque
highlands in
elegantly the shape of a pine   wind-twisted

half arch whether hillside or cliffside   +
i would not
go   I would not pass   so far beyond the drystone   but
how michael may dare venture   bear witness

like a gull so close to the wave
and I
noted my remove from this   from
dusk   spectral
settling upon his wings

claiming part of his
long, sunlit form then
as he was glancing back
i
met his eye   + quivering
easterly   there goes each dare
dear for parting by holidays and highways under a tame
                              evening's dimming cloud or dark

greens of pine or an hour hugging goodbye at the foot
of what was any other streetlamp

PS after a terrible beginning

I

brotherly / claimed go / once / the only television in the highlands / weary roll down / too it die / wherever the present participle ends / is it blood or blubbers / seal and kayak / was brave / seal will not brace / sea under / love / from crieff to criccieth crieth seal / seal takes a breath and says / salt air I go / and they have been around forever / now find / hats / be worn as socks / in the very west / there is something about barnacles / bird by seal / bird / for the worse / taught me that if / seating / I be ill / toward the sea refused / pretty and mixed / capeside / nor any more will

II

a long time ago is never lengthening my neck which I'm pretty sure precedes an obvious adduction of daddy long legs crumpled into a bathtub not so as the bathtub itself. Is it an arbitrary point that showerheads forewent the purple of the highlands and an anguilliform streak burnt rapidly? Contrary to popular humour some alpacas actually strive for a leg's length from showers, even keeping themselves so. For up to twenty minutes a jibe will take its toll and the tall might like to sit down where the water is colder, the pressure a little light.

acknowledgements

Thanks to the editors of the following publications, with whom some of these poems first appeared:

Amberflora
Minor Lit(s)
Poetry Wales
Sharkpack Poetry Review
Tentacular Magazine
Vanguard Editions

I am deeply grateful to Iris Colomb, Ali Graham, Mari Lavelle-Hill, Julia Rose Lewis, Lizzy Mossman, David Spittle, Owen Vince, Marion Wells for insight and feedback over many years; to Tiffany Atkinson, Andrea Holland, Laura Joyce, Sophie Robinson, and Philip Wilson, my teachers at UEA; and to my editor, Paul Hawkins.
AW

Andrew Wells has work in *Amberflora*, *3:AM Magazine*, *Minor Literature(s)*, *Poetry Wales*, *Fanzine*, and *The Scores*, among others. He is also the author of *J/W/U* (Pyramid, 2016). He is co-editor of HVTN Press

Hesterglock Press has a Patreon page. Patreon enables a regular pledge of your choice to artists, writers, musicians etc in return for special rewards & exclusives. Patreon's platform allows poets/artists like those behind Hesterglock Press to receive a steady revenue stream directly in contact with our readers. By signing-up and supporting us working in this way, you'll be helping to sustain an ongoing commitment to connecting with others, publishing radical & challenging books, collaborating with other artists and writers on projects that take risks & don't / won't make a million, but may make a difference or a change. Please support our publishing in return for free things like books, exclusive artworks and digital goodies. Take a look here https:// www.patreon.com/ hesterglock

With thanks to Elancharan Gunasekaran, who generously supports the work of Hesterglock Press and Paul Hawkins through Patreon, making this book & many others possible.

Forthcoming Hesterglock Press publications:

due 2020
The Perambulator- Should We Meet At The Crossroads, Keep Walking
SJ Fowler - Phoetry : Selected Photo Poems of SJ Fowler (collab. w/The Aleph)
Miggy Angel - The Poetarium
Neil Sparkes - Xerox Sonnets & X-Ray Blues
Lucy Furlong - clew (2nd edition)
Steve Ryan/Paul Hawkins - FLEA

due 2021
Vik Shirley - Disrupted Blue and other poems on Polaroid
SJ Fowler - Soft Rich Digital Ghosts; tweeting carparks dry
Bruno Neiva - Text Art 2010-2020
Rose Knapp - Tantric
Franco Cortese - ïï lí vì ei ii dì ei
Sarer Scotthorne - Meta Mutter

Printed in Poland
by Amazon Fulfillment
Poland Sp. z o.o., Wrocław